A Note to Parents

DK READERS is a compelling program for beginning readers, designed in conjunction with leading literacy experts, including Dr. Linda Gambrell, Professor of Education at Clemson University. Dr. Gambrell has served as President of the National Reading Conference and the College Reading Association, and has recently been elected to serve as President of the International Reading Association.

Beautiful illustrations and superb full-color photographs combine with engaging, easy-to-read stories to offer a fresh approach to each subject in the series. Each DK READER is guaranteed to capture a child's interest while developing his or her reading skills, general knowledge, and love of reading.

The five levels of DK READERS are aimed at different reading abilities, enabling you to choose the books that are exactly right for your child:

Pre-level 1: Learning to read
Level 1: Beginning to read
Level 2: Beginning to read alone
Level 3: Reading alone
Level 4: Proficient readers

The "normal" age at which a child begins to read can be anywhere from three to eight years old. Adult participation through the lower levels is very helpful for providing encouragement, discussing storylines, and sounding out unfamiliar words.

No matter which level you select, you can be sure that you are helping your child learn to read, then read to learn!

DK

LONDON, NEW YORK, MUNICH,
MELBOURNE, and DELHI

Series Editor Deborah Lock
Senior Art Editor Sonia Moore
U.S. Editor John Searcy
Production Georgina Hayworth
Picture Researcher Debra Weatherley
DTP Designer Emma Hansen
Jacket Designer Simon Oon

Reading Consultant
Linda Gambrell, Ph.D.

First American Edition, 2007
13 14 13 12 11 10 9 8
Published in the United States by DK Publishing
345 Hudson Street, New York, New York 10014
014-RD130-Feb/2007

Copyright © 2007 Dorling Kindersley Limited

Published in Great Britain by Dorling Kindersley Limited

DK books are available at special discounts when purchased in bulk
for sales promotions, premiums, fund-raising, or educational use.
For details, contact:
DK Publishing Special Markets
345 Hudson Street
New York, New York 10014
SpecialSales@dk.com

Library of Congress Cataloging-in-Publication Data
Lock, Deborah.
DK readers level 1 : submarines and submersibles / written by
Deborah Lock. -- 1st American ed., 2007. p. cm.
Includes bibliographical references and index.
ISBN: 978-0-7566-2550-4 (paperback)
ISBN: 978-0-7566-2551-1 (hardcover)
1. Submarines (Ships)--Juvenile literature. 2. Submersibles--Juvenile
literature. I. Title.
VM365.L63 2007
623.82'05--dc22

2006023679

Color reproduction by Colourscan, Singapore
Printed and bound in China by L Rex Printing Co., Ltd.

The publisher would like to thank the following for their kind
permission to reproduce their photographs:
Position key: a-above; b-below/bottom; c-center; l-left; r-right; t-top
2005 BAE Systems: 3b, 20-21c; Corbis: Mark Cooper 29r, 32cla;
Roger Ressmeyer 26; Getty Images: Torsten Blackwood / AFP 15b;
Randy Olson / National Geographic 18c; Jeff Rotman / Iconica 16-17c;
Brian Skerry 12-13c; Kurt Vinion 22b, 32tl; Image Quest Marine:
James D. Watt 10-11c; Jeff Rotman / jeffrotman.com: 2tr, 2t, 4c, 5b, 6l,
6-7c, 8-9c, 11t, 14c, 32clb; Navsource: Brian Nokell / US Navy Photo
24-25c, 30b, 32cl; Larry Smith / Defence Visual Information Center
22-23c, 27t, 28-29c; US Navy Photo 1br; Perry Slingsby Systems: 2br,
16t, 16b; Photolibrary: Purestock 30-31c; SMD Hydrovision: 2cr, 17cr;
Woods Hole Oceanographic Institition: 19b
All other images © Dorling Kindersley
For further information see: www.dkimages.com

Discover more at

www.dk.com

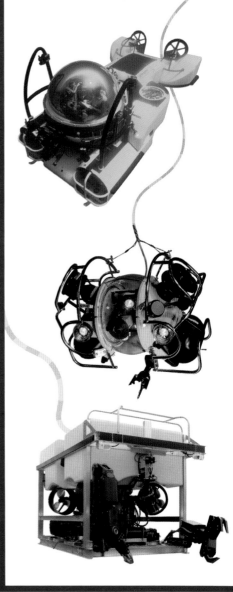

Contents

DK READERS

BEGINNING
1
TO READ

Submarines
and Submersibles

Written by Deborah Lock

DK Publishing

Down, down, down.
The submersible
[sub-MER-suh-bull]
dives under the sea.

Deeper, deeper, deeper.
A submersible is a craft used
for short trips deep underwater.
This submersible has
three people on board.

Jim, the pilot, steers
the submersible.
The computer screen
shows him where
to go.

computer
screen

Mark and Paul
look out
of the window.
They want to find out
about the sea floor.

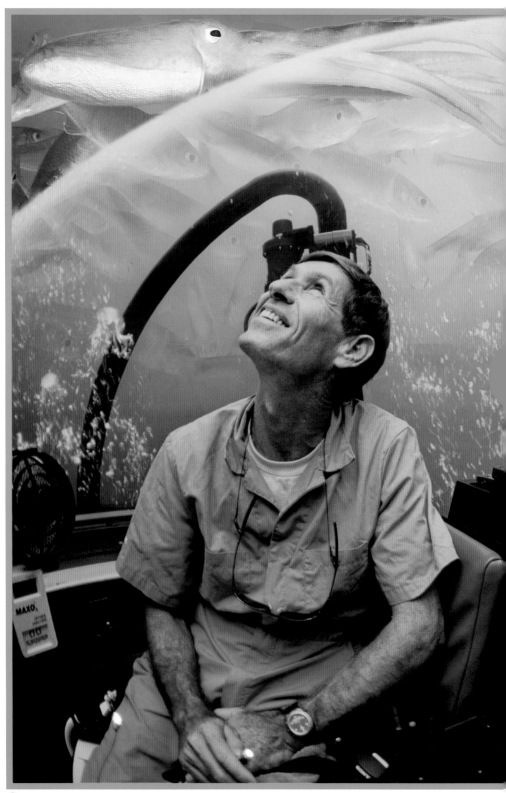

The submersible
reaches the sea floor.
The crew watches the sea animals.
"I can see an octopus," says Mark.
"Let's take a video of it."

They find
an underwater cave.
"Look at all the sharks,"
says Mark.
"This must be
where they rest."

The submersible
moves away along
the sea floor.

A strange shape appears
in front of them.
"What's that?" asks Jim.

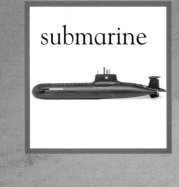

submarine

"It looks like the wreck
of an old war submarine
[sub-MUH-reen]," says Paul.
"We'd better get going," says Jim.
"The water's getting rough."

Jim steers the submersible
to the surface.
A crane lifts it out of the water.

"We can send the underwater
robot to look at the wreck,"
says Paul.

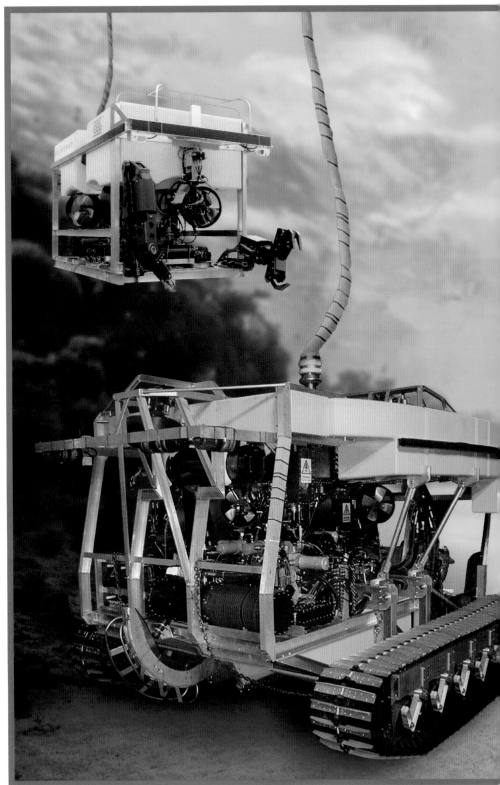

Robot submersibles,
or ROVs, are used when
the water is dangerous.
They are used to
explore the sea floor
and wrecks.

ROVs can also be used
to lay cables and mend
pipes deep underwater.

The ROV is lowered
into the water.
It has a cable line
linking it
to the ship.

Jim controls the ROV
from the ship and steers it
around the wreck.
It sends back pictures of
the submarine.

Modern submarines can carry more than 120 people. They are often used for long trips underwater.

Many submarines are painted
black so it is hard to see them
in the dark water.

This submarine is docked
in a harbor.
The crew gets the submarine
ready to leave.

hatch

Then they climb inside.
"Close the hatches,"
orders the captain.

The submarine moves away
from the dock.
Out at sea, the submarine
dives below the waves.
It will be at sea for three months.

The crew takes turns eating,
working, and sleeping.
Their beds are bunks.

Some members of the crew
work in the control room.
After three months underwater,
they take the submarine
up to the surface.

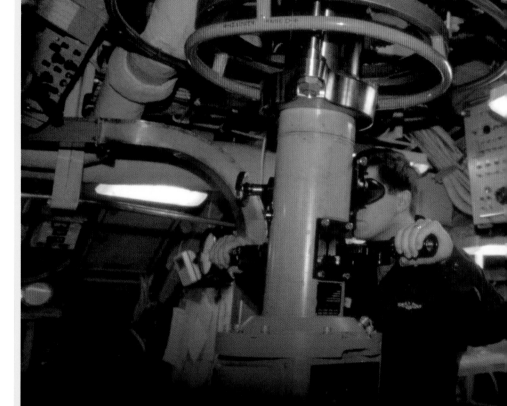

The captain needs to make sure
it is safe to surface.
The periscopes [PARE-uh-scopes]
are raised just above the water.

periscope

The men look through
the eyepieces.
The mirrors inside the periscopes
show them what is on the surface.

The men can see the coast.

They are almost home.

"Surface," the captain orders.

Up, up, up.

sail

The submarine's sail appears first.
The submarine makes a big wave
as it rises.
SWOOSH!

Glossary

Computer screen a surface that shows pictures

Hatch an opening used to get into a submarine

Periscope a long tube used to see above the water

Sail the raised part of a submarine

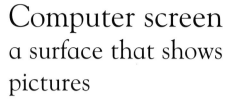

Submarine a craft that can travel underwater